Dear Parents and Educators,

Our 500 Questions Game Book was created for parents and children to have fun together while learning. The book presents material on math, literacy, science, music, social skills, nature, creativity and health – all fundamental to school success. Our questions are lively, enriching and unique, and our bonus riddles add extra learning and laughter!

Building a child's confidence and enthusiasm for learning at an early age is key to future success. It is our sincere hope that the Learnalots™ will inspire children, and those who care for them, to learn something new every day.

– The BrightStart Learning Team

Is length measured in inches or pounds?

Does wool come from pigs or sheep?

Are diamond rings sparkly or sprinkly?

inches, sheep, sparkly

Is a group of birds
called a smock or a flock?

Is a blizzard a
really bad snowstorm or
a really bad rainstorm?

Are tires made of
rubber or plastic?

flock, snowstorm, rubber

3

Are dinosaurs still living
or extinct?

Are mittens made out of
string or yarn?

Do astronauts travel
on comets or in rockets?

extinct, yarn, rockets

Are racing sleds pulled by husky dogs or polar bears?

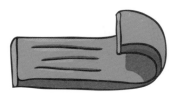

Are s'mores made with chocolate and marshmallows or chocolate and maple syrup?

Is the sun a star or a moon?

Do eyebrows protect your nose or your eyes?

Does a rhinoceros have a horn or an antler?

Is the weather at the equator hot or cold?

eyes, horn, hot

Do snails slide or glide?

Which color mixed with white makes pink: blue or red?

Is our galaxy named the Milky Way or the Chocolate Chip?

slide, red, Milky Way

Are doors shaped like rectangles or ovals?

Do blueberries grow on trees or bushes?

Which are good luck: three-leaf clovers or four-leaf clovers?

rectangles, bushes, four-leaf

Do superheroes have
X-ray vision or X-ray smelling?

Does stiff mean
flexible or inflexible?

Are rainbows shaped
like arcs or zig zags?

Do magicians say
Abracadabra or Obracadobra?

Do germs make you
sick or healthy?

If you dig deep into the
ground, are you likely to
find water or seaweed?

abracadabra, sick, water

? ?

Why can't Tyrannosaurus rexes clap?

?

?

?

They are
extinct!

When lava is inside the earth, is it called magma or magenta?

Do fireflies glow at night or at noon?

Do princesses wear jewels or jelly beans?

magma, at night, jewels

What closes at the end
of a play: the window
or the curtain?

Does reverse mean
go backwards or go forwards?

Does camouflage mean
to hide or to show off?

curtain, go backwards, to hide

Do polar bears live at the north pole or the south pole?

What floats in water: a stick or a brick?

Are luaus a tradition from the state of Hawaii or the state of Ohio?

Do you eat breakfast
when the sun rises or
when the sun sets?

Which is a
symbol of love:
a heart or
a circle?

Do snakes hiss or huffle?

sun rises, heart, hiss

Is a tortoise a type of turtle or a type of snail?

What is used to make salad: sausage or spinach?

Is the sun really close or really far away?

Do spiders make
webs or nests?

Is is polite to sneeze into
your shirt sleeve or your
pant pocket?

What do people eat
when they are sick:
chicken soup or candy canes?

webs, shirt sleeve, chicken soup

Does magnify mean: make bigger or make smaller?

Do grapes grow on vines or trees?

How many poles does the earth have: one or two?

Does a duck have
a frill or a bill?

Does cold air rise or sink?

Is the outside of a seed
called a shell or a coat?

bill, sink, shell

 Which flower do people blow on when making a wish: a dandelion or daffodil?

What day of the week comes after Friday: Sunday or Saturday?

Which has a hard shell: a snail or a slug?

Are ghost stories told around a campfire or a barbecue?

What can sunshine and rain create: lightning or a rainbow?

Does "prepare" mean to get ready or to slow down?

campfire, rainbow, get ready

? ?

What kind
of room has
no doors or
windows?

? ?

A
mushroom!

Is a dragonfly a bird or insect?

Do alarm clocks wake you up
or put you to sleep?

Are the Niagara Falls large
waterfalls or large snowfalls?

insect, wake you up, waterfalls

When you work at a job, do you get paid with money or hugs?

Are cartwheels done in gymnastics or golf?

Is a sea turtle a reptile or a fish?

money, gymnastics, reptile

Do ladybugs eat cupids or aphids?

Is an alligator a fish or a reptile?

Are pyramids located in
Egypt or Alaska?

aphids, reptile, Egypt

Who has antlers:
elk or rhinoceroses?

How many legs do all
insects have: six or eight?

Is soil the upper layer
of the Earth's surface
or the bottom layer?

elk, six, upper

Are unicorns real or imaginary?

Do apples have pits or cores?

When you see a silly movie,
do you laugh or cry?

real, cores, laugh

Do people pull carrots out of the ground or pick them from trees?

Do birds fly south or north in the winter?

Which animal can hide inside its shell: a hermit crab or a lobster?

ground, south, hermit crab

Does a parrot have
a beak or lips?

Are islands surrounded
by water or quicksand?

Do people snore through
their ears or their noses?

Is a group of bees called
a swarm or a cluster?

Is a baby sheep called
a lamb or a calf?

What do people use
to jump out of planes:
parachutes or parakeets?

swarm, lamb, parachutes

Is the Great Wall in
France or China?

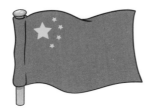

When you light a candle,
does it melt or boil?

Is hockey played on ice
or in a pool?

China, melt, on ice

Do pumpkins grow on trees
or on vines in the ground?

Where would you find
a cactus: in the desert
or in the swamp?

Do mean words
make you feel
happy or sad?

vines, desert, sad

? ?

What two things can never be eaten for breakfast?

?

?

Lunch

and

Dinner!

Do horses gallop or wallop?

Does hot water boil or spoil?

Are boats made out of material that is buoyant or non-buoyant?

Which of these strengthens
your stomach muscles:
laughing or burping?

Which is sour:
a lime or a carrot?

Does every country have a
different flag or a
different blanket?

laughing, lime, flag

Do anchors keep boats in place or help them move?

Do vampires have sharp toes or sharp teeth?

Are pupils in your eyes or ears?

keep in place, teeth, eyes

Does exercise speed up your hair growth or your heart rate?

Is hail frozen rain or frozen rocks?

Do cactuses contain water or glue?

heart rate, frozen rain, water

Do you paint on a
canvas or a caravan?

Does the moon sometimes
look like a heart or a crescent?

Is paper made from
trees or from fruit?

When do plants grow faster: the summer or the winter?

Which is made with milk: ice cream or chicken soup?

Is the color orange a mix of yellow and red or purple and red?

Are skyscrapers buildings or airplanes?

Which organ pumps blood through our bodies: the heart or the lungs?

Is ice falling from the sky called hail or kale?

buildings, heart, hail

43

Do you leave teeth for the
Tooth Fairy under your bed
or under your pillow?

Is gingerbread made with
molasses or marshmallows?

Do cows clean theirs noses with
their tongues or their hooves?

pillow, molasses, tongues

Do cats like to eat
apples or tuna fish?

Do skateboards have
four wheels or six?

Are porcupines soft or prickly?

If you add white paint to blue paint, does it become dark blue or light blue?

Do you catch butterflies with a fishing pole or a net?

Are cycles with three wheels called quadcycles or tricycles?

light blue, net, tricycles

What has
four wheels
and flies?

A
garbage
truck!

Do kings live in castles or caves?

Does stealing make you happy or sad?

Which animals can walk upside down: spiders or mice?

castles, sad, spiders

Does chocolate come from cocoa beans or carrots?

Do allergies make you sneeze or giggle?

Is glass made from sand or dirt?

cocoa beans, sneeze, sand

Do parrots live in
cold or tropical climates?

Do pigs roll in mud to
get dirty or to keep cool?

Does harvest mean
to collect or to spread out?

tropical, keep cool, collect

Was Tyrannosaurus rex a carnivore or herbivore?

Does blinking help keep our eyes wet or dry?

Are elves short or tall?

carnivore, wet, short

If you are behind the person in third place, are you in second or fourth place?

Does the name rhinoceros mean thick skin or nose horn?

Are butterfly wings symmetrical or asymmetrical?

fourth, nose horn, symmetrical

Was pizza invented
in Italy or Russia?

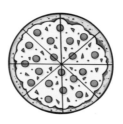

Does nocturnal
mean: active
during the day
or active at night?

Which ocean animal lives in a
shell: a clam or a seahorse?

Italy, active at night, clam

What part of
a plant grows
underground:
the stem
or roots?

Do recipes tell you how to cook
food or how to build something?

Is karate a sport or a card game?

roots, cook food, sport

Is sushi made with beef or fish?

Does the Earth
rotate or stay still?

Which object can make a sound
like the ocean: a shell or a rock?

fish, rotate, shell

Are dreams in your
heart or in your brain?

Are chimneys
made of brick
or wood?

Is the Mississippi a big river
or a big waterfall?

brain, brick, river

57

Do pilots
fly planes or
fix planes?

How many months are
in a year: 14 or 12?

Do raisins come from
grapes or oranges?

fly planes, 12, grapes

Why is
6 afraid of 7?

Because
7, 8, 9!

Do plants need darkness
or sunlight to grow?

Which carnival ride takes you
upside down: a roller coaster
or a Ferris wheel?

What is it called when
you roll on the ground:
a somersault or a superloop?

sunlight, roller-coaster, somersault

Which hatches from an egg:
a snake or a mouse?

What has the same meaning as
"kind": generous or greedy?

Which bird is bigger:
a hummingbird or a turkey?

snake, generous, turkey

Which food is usually eaten
at a baseball game:
hot dogs or hash browns?

Which food makes
your bones grow:
milk or lemonade?

When something tastes
yummy, is it called
delicious or detectable?

Is a group of fish called
a school or a library?

Do eggs need to stay warm
or cold before they hatch?

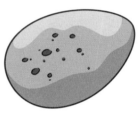

Is a penguin
a bird or
a fish?

school, warm, bird

Do captains steer
boats or race cars?

Which shape has only three
corners: a square or a triangle?

What would you use to
measure the length of a
caterpillar: a ruler or a scale?

boats, triangle, ruler

Are traditional
Japanese robes
called kimonos
or kayaks?

Is the moon larger or
smaller than the Earth?

Does canine refer to
a dog or a cat?

kimonos, smaller, dog

Do octopuses have
eight arms or ten arms?

What part of lettuce do we eat:
the root or the leaves?

Does a seal have flippers or fins?

eight, leaves, flippers

What is the name of the world's largest desert: Sarah or Sahara?

Is the ocean filled with salt water or fresh water?

Which rocks are best for skipping: flat and smooth or big and round?

Sahara, salt water, flat and smooth

Does lying make you
feel happy or sad?

Is a duck an amphibian or a bird?

Is the strongest muscle in our
bodies the tongue or the bicep?

sad, bird, tongue

How many states are in the
United States: 50 or 60?

Do roller coasters make
you dizzy or frizzy?

Does dust make you
sneeze or giggle?

50, dizzy, sneeze

? ?

Where do
library books
like to sleep?

?

?

Under their
covers!

Is the Great Barrier Reef
in Australia or in Africa?

Does stretch mean
lengthen or shorten?

Do fevers make your body
heat up or cool down?

Which bird is nocturnal:
a robin or an owl?

Does exercise
make your
muscles stronger
or weaker?

Are there four or five
seasons in a year?

owl, stronger, four

Do kangaroos hop or skip?

Do spiders have
eight legs or six?

Are ears made out of
bone or cartilage?

hop, eight, cartilage

Do you use your arms
or your legs to jump?

Do reptiles have scales or hair?

Do batteries store power
or calculate speed?

legs, scales, store power

Do friends make you
smile or sneeze?

Which of these is a weather
word: fizzle or blizzard?

Which fruit has more vitamin C:
an apple or an orange?

Is a baby deer called
a fawn or fan?

How many scoops
are in a triple
ice cream cone?

Which vegetable makes you cry:
onions or artichokes?

fawn, three, onions

Does syrup come from
trees or flowers?

As you go up in the sky,
does it get hotter or colder?

When people wake up,
do they stretch or sneeze?

trees, colder, stretch

Which is the tallest
mountain in the world:
Mt. Everest or Mt. Rainer?

Do caterpillars sleep
in cradles or cocoons?

What color are tree leaves
in the fall: orange or blue?

Mt. Everest, cocoons, orange

Which of these is unique
to you: your fingerprint
or your elbow print?

Does a clock keep track
of time or speed?

Which sense do you use
when you listen to music:
taste or hearing?

fingerprint, time, hearing

81

If you cut a watermelon
in half, how many pieces
do you have: two or four?

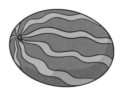

Does a kangaroo carry its
baby in a pouch or a purse?

Does separate mean to
bring together or break apart?

two, pouch, break apart

What is a tree's favorite drink?

Root beer!

Do leopards sleep
in trees or in caves?

Does toss mean to kick something
or to throw something?

Which color of car gets hotter
in the sun: a black car
or a white car?

trees, throw, black

Which of these animals don't have legs: eels or eagles?

How many seconds are in a minute: sixty or eighty?

Which sense is used when looking at a picture: sight or hearing?

eels, sixty, sight

Are trolls real creatures
or imaginary creatures?

Do Eskimos live in the
desert or the arctic?

Do people scuba dive with
a snorkel or with an air tank?

imaginary, arctic, air tank

Is a tepee a type of
tent or a log house?

Is spaghetti eaten with
meatballs or meatloaf?

When you catch a
snowflake with your tongue,
does it melt or freeze?

tent, meatballs, melt

Does August come before
or after September?

Is butter made from
cow's milk or pig's milk?

Do people catch fish
with carrots or worms?

before, cow's milk, worms

Are skates used to play
soccer or to play hockey?

What color are tree leaves
in the spring: red or green?

Which sport is played with
a bat: football or baseball?

hockey, green, baseball

Are constellations recognizable sky patterns made by planets or stars?

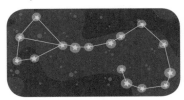

What do tadpoles turn into: frogs or turtles?

Do janitors clean bathrooms or fly planes?

stars, frogs, clean bathrooms

91

Is it easier to run in
sneakers or snow shoes?

Are computers used for designing
airplanes or making cookies?

Does wise mean
silly or smart?

sneakers, designing airplanes, smart

Is Go Fish a card game
or board game?

Do penguins waddle or wibble?

Is a stop sign shaped
like a square or octagon?

card game, waddle, octagon

Are eggs oval or square?

Does a cactus have spines or whiskers?

Who is a princess's father: the king or the prince?

oval, spines, king

What is the same size and shape as an elephant, but weighs nothing?

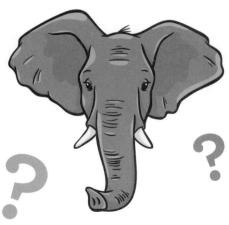

Its
shadow!

Is a telescope used to help see things that are far away or close up?

Do balloons filled with helium rise or sink?

Is a baby cow called a calf or a cub?

far away, rise, calf

Which of these is
a symptom of a cold:
warm ears or a runny nose?

Do people ski wearing
swimsuits or snow jackets?

Is a kiwi a fruit or vegetable?

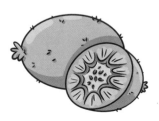

runny nose, snow jackets, fruit

What do people toss into a wishing well for good luck: rocks or pennies?

What comes after Kindergarten, Preschool or First Grade?

Do panda bears eat blueberries or bamboo?

Does a snorkel let you
breathe underwater
or smell flowers?

Where are you more likely
to see a submarine:
in a pond or in an ocean?

Which of these is a lunch food:
pancakes or sandwiches?

breathe underwater, ocean, sandwiches

Do veterinarians take care
of animals or people?

Do ladybugs have
stripes or spots?

Are most pies made out
of vegetables or fruit?

Do leprechauns or gnomes
hide gold at the
end of a rainbow?

What has a hard shell:
a crab or an octopus?

Is origami an Italian tradition
or a Japanese tradition?

leprechauns, crab, Japanese

Does a conductor drive a train or cook food?

In which sport do you knock over pins with a ball: bowling or golf?

What color is watermelon when it is ripe: green or pink?

Are feather boas
fancy or flabby?

Does hibernate mean to sleep
or run around in circles?

Do scales measure
weight or height?

fancy, sleep, weight

If you want to see clowns and acrobats, would you go to an opera or a circus?

How many eggs are in a dozen: 10 or 12?

Which word ends with the letter G: kiss or hug?

Do tires have treads or threads?

Do bees sting with their noses or their butts?

Is the largest rainforest on Earth called the Amazon or the Amazing?

treads, butts, Amazon

Why does a flamingo lift up one leg?

Because if it
lifted up both
legs, it would
fall over!

Do doctors go to
law school or medical school?

Which fruits are purple:
grapes or watermelon?

Is honey made by
bees or butterflies?

medical school, grapes, bees

Is a tornado fast moving wind or fast moving water?

Are flippers used in pools or bathtubs?

Is there a famous bike race called the Tires de France or Tour de France?

wind, pools, Tour de France

Are computers powered by gasoline or electricity?

Are olives salty or sweet?

Do plants grow in soil or salt?

Do coconuts grow on
pine trees or palm trees?

Is an animal that
makes its own shell called
a mollusk or sheltie?

What means the same
as "start": begin or finish?

palm, mollusk, begin

Does supersonic mean
really fast or really slow?

Which food makes your eyes
strong: carrots or cupcakes?

Is the color green
a mix of blue and yellow
or blue and purple?

fast, carrots, blue and yellow

Which holiday has
fireworks: Fourth of July
or St. Patrick's Day?

Which lives underground:
worms or grasshoppers?

Which vegetable comes
in different colors:
peppers or peas?

Fourth of July, worms, peppers

Are unicorns similar to horses or beavers?

Which do you cook on a stove: cupcakes or spaghetti sauce?

Does lunar refer to the sun or the moon?

What is larger:
a hill or a mountain?

Do cactuses have
flowers or feathers?

Which of these islands
is part of the United States:
Hawaii or Jamaica?

mountain, flowers, Hawaii

Is the equator a line around the middle of earth or something you ride on in a building?

What is healthier to drink: soda or water?

When you climb a very tall mountain is it hot or cold at the top?

What vegetable is used to make guacamole: broccoli or avocado?

What would you eat at a Japanese restaurant: sushi or lasagna?

What gas makes up 75% of the sun's mass: helium or hydrogen?

avocado, sushi, hydrogen

Why was the broom late?

It
over-swept!

Which grows underground:
a sweet potato or a zucchini?

Does food last longer in the
refrigerator or the freezer?

Which of these foods
belong to the dairy group:
cabbage or cheese?

sweet potato, freezer, cheese

What will help you
go to sleep: playing a game
or listening to a story?

Who would be more
likely to use a
thermometer at work:
a plumber or a doctor?

Which food is healthier for you:
french fries or carrots?

story, doctor, carrots

Which activity will keep you healthy: watching TV or playing at the park?

Which is smaller: a lake or an ocean?

Which food makes your bones strong: meat or milk?

Does brushing your teeth
prevent cavities or
prevent capillaries?

Which organ
helps you breathe:
your stomach
or your lungs?

What is the first day
of the school week:
Wednesday or Monday?

cavities, lungs, Monday

Is a toad more like a fish
or more like a frog?

Which word ends in
a SH sound: fish or fly?

SH

What rhymes with tree:
flea or tray?

Are peas a kind of
fruit or vegetable?

How many pennies make
one dollar: 1,000 or 100?

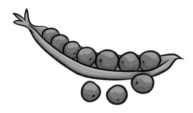

Which word means something
you do when you are tired:
pest or rest?

vegetable, 100, rest

Do you eat corn on a cob or corn on a pod?

Which is worth more: a nickel or a penny?

What do you call an old animal bone that has turned into rock: a skeleton or a fossil?

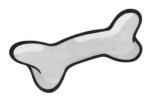

cob, nickel, fossil

What do you leave behind
you when you walk:
footprints or tire tracks?

Which of
these is in
outer space:
an oil well or
a black hole?

What do you call a car with
sirens that takes you to the
hospital: an ambulance or a taxi?

footprints, black hole, ambulance

What do you use to paddle a kayak: a spatula or an oar?

Is a quilt a kind of rug or a kind of blanket?

Is a woodpecker a type of bird or a type of tree?

oar, blanket, bird

129

Which word has the letter B
in it: around or about?

B

Do salmon swim upstream
or downstream when they
are leaving the ocean?

How many syllables does the word
"dictionary" have: three or four?

about, upstream, four

What is full
of holes but
can still hold
water?

A
sponge!

Which word has the letter E in it: bee or bug?

E

Does the word "habitat" refer to where an animal lives or how an animal behaves?

Which is heavier: a balloon filled with water or a balloon filled with air?

bee, where it lives, water

133

Which is worth more:
a nickel or a quarter?

Which is a kind of bird:
an otter or an ostrich?

If you have seven apples and
give three away, how many
do you have left: two or four?

quarter, ostrich, four

Which is a kind of cat:
a llama or a leopard?

Which would you wear on your
head: a watch or a wig?

Which is larger:
a thousand or a million?

leopard, wig, million

What do you call rock that is so hot that it has melted: mud or lava?

Did stegosaurus dinosaurs eat meat or plants?

What is smaller: a trumpet or a tuba?

lava, plants, trumpet

Which can you use to listen to music: headphones or earplugs?

Which sport do you enjoy in the winter: skiing or baseball?

On which holiday do people dye eggs: Thanksgiving or Easter?

headphones, skiing, Easter

What do you need to fly
a kite: rain or wind?

Which kind of bird can talk:
a sparrow or a parrot?

Which object
helps you
swim fast:
flip flops or
flippers?

wind, parrot, flippers

Which can run faster:
a person or a horse?

Which animal sleeps upside-down
in a cave: an owl or a bat?

What kind of animal used to be
a tadpole: a fish or a frog?

Which food is crunchy:
celery or tomatoes?

What do
pine trees
produce: acorns
or pine cones?

Do pennies float or sink in water?

celery, pine cones, sink

Is the harp
an instrument
of the
percussion family
or the
string family?

Which is larger:
a mouse or a rat?

Who is older:
your mother
or your
grandmother?

What is left over after you burn a log: ashes or rocks?

Which two numbers add up to 20: 12 and 4 or 11 and 9?

What month comes before December: November or January?

Where do snowmen go to dance?

A snow ball!

If you wanted to visit Antarctica, would you need a car or a boat?

Which animal do farmers use to protect their livestock: dogs or cats?

Are pretzels a form of baked bread or a lemon flavored candy?

boat, dogs, baked bread

Does the early bird get
the worm or the germ?

When is there more sun:
in the summer or the winter?

Which is helpful when you
get lost: a recipe or a map?

worm, summer, map

What is a game you might
play at a birthday party:
pin the tail or trick-or-treat?

What is usually cooked on a
grill: hamburgers or meatballs?

Which is thicker:
ketchup or milk?

pin the tail, hamburgers, ketchup

Which do you cook in the oven:
a cake or soup?

Which word starts with
the letter K: toy or kite?

K

What is the most eaten fruit
in the world: apples or mangoes?

cake, kite, mangoes

What do you eat at school: lunch or dinner?

What are you watching if you see tutus: a ballet or an opera?

What do you call a large group of people playing instruments: a trio or a band?

lunch, ballet, band

What month comes after
March: August or April?

How many continents are
there on Earth: seven or ten?

What is harder:
a diamond or chalk?

April, seven, diamond

Is the number 12
odd or even?

12

How long does it take
you to brush your teeth:
two minutes or two hours?

Which costs more:
a teddy bear or a car?

even, two minutes, car

151

Which word starts with the letter C: kite or cat?

Are rain clouds made out of smoke or water?

Is lederhosen a traditional Scottish or German outfit?

cat, water, German

Which word rhymes with
soup: troop or sour?

Is a paper clip one inch long
or one foot long?

Do we measure height
in feet or grams?

troop, one inch, feet

What would weigh about one pound: a loaf of bread or a slice of bread?

Is a caterpillar closer to an inch or foot in length?

What is larger: a cup or a gallon?

a loaf, an inch, gallon

What gets
wetter the
more it dries?

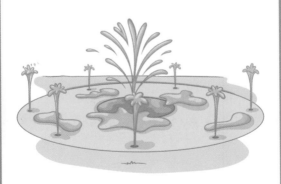

A
towel!

If it is 80 degrees
Fahrenheit outside,
is it hot or cold?

Should you protect your
eyes when you look at the
moon or the sun?

Which is worth less:
a dime or a quarter?

Do you see your shadow better on sunny days or cloudy days?

Do deer eat plants or meat?

Which month comes after January: February or March?

sunny, plants, February

How many inches are
in a foot: 12 or 20?

Which word rhymes with rough:
cough or tough?

Where is the water colder:
on the ocean surface
or on the ocean bottom?

12, tough, ocean bottom

Which word has the same vowel sound as ski: sky or street?

What do you call an animal that eats meat: a carnivore or an herbivore?

Are snowflakes all identical to one another or unique to one another?

street, carnivore, unique

If you have five nickels,
how much money do you have:
25 cents or 50 cents?

What shape is a cardboard
box: a sphere or a cube?

What shape is a drum:
a sphere or a cylinder?

25 cents, cube, cylinder

How many bases are there in a baseball diamond: four or five?

Do dogs like to catch sticks or stones?

Is the number seven odd or even?

four, sticks, odd

What is the largest organ of the human body: the stomach or the skin?

Do sailboats have masts or blasts to hold their sails?

What brings you down when you jump: gravy or gravity?

skin, masts, gravity

Do most birds lay eggs
in the spring or fall?

Which is faster:
a boat or a plane?

What colors are on the
American flag: red, white, and
green, or red, white, and blue?

spring, plane, red, white, and blue

Does lunch come
before or after breakfast?

Which holds more water:
a bathtub or a sink?

Which has ink in it:
a marker or a pencil?

after, bathtub, marker

What emerges
from a chrysalis:
a bird or
a butterfly?

Which makes light from a flame:
a light bulb or a candle?

Which uses more energy:
jumping up and down
or lying on the ground?

butterfly, candle, jumping

What has
two hands,
a round face,
always runs,
but stays in
one place?

A
clock!

What is a good topping for ice cream: chocolate sauce or tomato sauce?

Do you use your arms or legs to give hugs?

Which can grow taller: a bush or a tree?

chocolate sauce, arms, tree

Do lions eat plants or meat?

Which year is closer to today: 2010 or 1910?

Which word has the same vowel sound as pear: fair or fear?

meat, 2010, fair

What is another name
for a shooting star:
a meteorite or an asteroid?

Which instrument is shaped like a
circle: a tambourine or a guitar?

Where is it safer during a
lightning storm: inside a house
or in a swimming pool?

meteorite, tambourine, inside a house

Is a tsunami a giant wave in the ocean or a tropical disease?

Do you keep ice cream in the refrigerator or the freezer?

Which word is one you would find in music: a chord or a court?

wave, freezer, chord

Do you play the drums with drumstones or drumsticks?

What do you call a scientist who studies the weather: a meteorologist or a zoologist?

Are pumpkins ripe in the spring or the fall?

Do you build a snowman in the summer or the winter?

Are bongos a type of drum or a type of clothing?

Are pennies made of rubber or metal?

winter, drum, metal

What can you add to baking soda to make it bubble: water or vinegar?

Do millipedes or centipedes have more legs?

Are polar bears good swimmers or bad swimmers?

Which sport is played
with bouncy orange balls:
basketball or bowling?

Which is the most used letter in
the alphabet: the E or the K?

E K

Is a tree living or non-living?

basketball, E, living

What rhymes with snake:
snake or rake?

Which can absorb more water:
paper or plastic?

Is the sun larger or smaller
than the earth?

rake, paper, larger

Which name ends in the letter M: Tyler or Tim?

M

Which goes around in a circle: a carousel or a swing?

If you dive deep under water, is there more or less light?

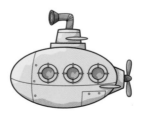

Tim, carousel, less light

What do you call a dog in the desert?

A
hot dog!

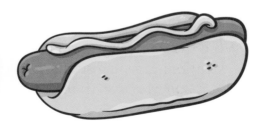

Do lemons taste spicy or tart?

Is a piccolo a small fruit
or a small flute?

Which is the longer school
vacation: spring vacation
or summer vacation?

tart, small flute, summer

What is the
opposite direction
of north:
west or south?

Which part of the map tells
you which direction is north:
the legend or the compass?

What is a food made at
an outdoor barbecue:
hot dogs or oatmeal?

south, compass, hot dogs

Does butter get hard or soft when it is very cold?

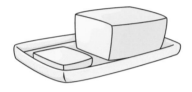

Is it faster to boil water on the stove or in the oven?

During cold winters, do bees eat flower nectar or saved honey?

hard, stove, honey

What kind of fruit is heavy and brown: a banana or a pineapple?

Which has slower moving water: a creek or a river?

Which word has more syllables: unicorn or popcorn?

pineapple, river, unicorn

Which word has more letters:
Missouri or Mississippi?

ABC

Which instrument
makes a
deeper sound:
a tuba or
a trumpet?

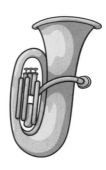

Is Big Ben a clock tower
in England or Spain?

Mississippi, tuba, England

185

What protects your skin
from the sun: hand lotion
or sunscreen?

Who uses a stethoscope:
a dentist or a doctor?

What is the name of the
longest bone in your body:
the femur or the fibula?

sunscreen, doctor, femur

Do magicians make rabbits disappear or dance?

What sport are you playing if you have a stick and a puck: golf or hockey?

Which tree loses its leaves every fall: a pine tree or an oak tree?

disappear, hockey, oak tree

Where on the earth is it colder: at the poles or at the equator?

Which word rhymes with neigh: fly or play?

Are mammals who carry their young in pouches called Martians or marsupials?

poles, play, marsupials

Where did Cleopatra live: in France or in Egypt?

Do rainbows appear when there is sun and fog or when there is sun and snow?

Is a boa a type of lizard or a type of snake?

Egypt, sun and fog, snake

How many sides does an octagon have: seven or eight?

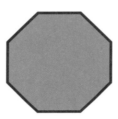

Which month is the shortest: September or February?

JUNE

Does an octopus give birth or lay eggs?

eight, February, lay eggs

How do you fix a broken pumpkin?

With a
pumpkin
patch!

Is a young swan called
a cyclops or a cygnet?

Is brown frosting usually vanilla
flavored or chocolate flavored?

Why are giraffe
tongues black:
to prevent insect
bites or to prevent
sunburn?

Which American holiday
is always on a Thursday?

Which of these objects float:
apples or rocks?

Is the air around the Earth
called the atmosphere
or the hemisphere?

Thanksgiving, apples, atmosphere

Which flower
has thorns:
a tulip or a rose?

Which of these is not an insect:
a ladybug or a spider?

Do computers get
colds or viruses?

rose, spider, viruses

Is the Earth covered mostly by water or mostly by land?

Which of these is a type of cow: Jersey or Geronimo?

Do woodpeckers drill holes into trees to find nuts or to find insects?

water, Jersey, catch insects

What color is the sky
when it rains: purple or grey?

Is a joey a baby skunk
or baby kangaroo?

What color are tree leaves
in the fall: orange or green?

grey, kangaroo, orange

Do you dig a hole using
a hammer or a shovel?

Does the big hand on a clock
point to the hour or the minute?

Which animal has a pink
curly tail: a bear or a pig?

shovel, minute, pig

Which vehicle blows a whistle:
a race car or a train?

Do kids put their school supplies
in a backpack or paper bag?

How many syllables does the
word "tomato" have: two or three?

train, backpack, three

Are thin pancakes
called crepes or croissants?

Are pumpkins picked
in the fall or spring?

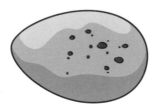

Which of these animals
doesn't hatch from an egg:
a snake or a seal?

crepes, fall, seal